Under The Moon
A Kid's Guide To Norway Fjords

Photography by John D. Weigand
Poetry by Penelope Dyan

Bellissima Publishing, LLC
Jamul, California
www.bellissimapublishing.com

Copyright © 2017 by Penny D. Weigand and John D. Weigand

All rights reserved. No part of this book may be reproduced or transmitted in any form or by any means, electronic or mechanical, including photocopying, recording, or by any other means, or by any information or storage retrieval system, without permission from the publisher.

ISBN 978-1-61477-274-3
First Edition

"The earth laughs in flowers."

Ralph Waldo Emerson

Under The Moon
Bellissima Publishing, LLC

Introduction

A fjord is a long and narrow inlet with steep sides and cliffs created by geological glacial erosion. There are many, many fjords that you can find along the coasts of Alaska as well as British Columbia, Chile, Greenland and Iceland, You can also find fjords on the Kerguelen Islands, in New Zealand, Norway, Labrador, Nunavut, Newfoundland, and Washington state! However, in this case, our author and photographer hopped on the ferry boat at Flam, Norway and headed out to see the famous fjords of Norway. But no matter where you are, and whether you travel through the pages of this book, or you travel in person to far off places, one thing is very clear; and that is that, like the geological make up of this great planet of ours, we are more alike than we are different, and we should embrace our differences as well as how we are alike, because we all live under the very same sun and moon.

Use this book by the award wining author, attorney and former teacher, Penelope Dyan, and photographer John D. Weigand to practice reading skills as you turn the pages of this book. When you are finished, watch the free music video that goes along with this book on Bellissimavideo's YouTube channel. And remember when learning is fun, kids love to learn!

Under The Moon
Bellissima Publishing, LLC

Under The Moon
A Kid's Guide To Norway Fjords

Photography by John D. Weigand
Poetry by Penelope Dyan

You board the Ferry at the Flam dock.
Mom says, "We're early.
I checked the clock."
Dad says,
"It's better to be early
rather than late."
Mom complains,
"Now we'll have to wait!"

But not before too long
you are sailing on your way.
A beautiful sea gull in the sky
seems to lead the way.

Past four houses of red you float.
Dad takes a photograph
from the top deck of the boat.

Next you see two houses of white, where two Norwegian families sleep at night.

And even more houses are ahead,
far more houses,
than those first four houses of red.
And right before your eyes
are seen,
lovely homes in a valley green.

And then you see it,
like a photograph of black and white.
You wonder and ask,
"Dad, is it scary here at night?"
Dad says,
"Nighttime will be coming here soon.
And just like home, they have the moon.
And when all is said and done,
when daybreak comes,
they'll have the sun!"

Dad snaps a photograph
of another fjord too!
Mom says,
"The world is more alike than different."
You agree and say, "That's true!"
Then Dad says,
"You would never want to look or act exactly like your very best friend. And your differences don't mean you'd want your friendship to end."
Mom then says,
"Differences are the spice of life!
And then you agree and you say,
"You are right!"

And as the water shimmers,
and as by another home you float past,
you really hope this day will last!
Even though you know
as down this waterway you wend,
that all good things,
eventually must come to their end.

And then, right out of the blue,
a motorboat motors
right past YOU!
And your mother thoughtfully says,
because SHE is wise,
"Sometimes you need to look
with your heart,
and NOT through your eyes."

And you think about all of the houses,
of this crowded looking little town.
And then you look up at Mom and Dad,
and you look ALL around.
It is very, very cold today in Norway,
but you have had a lot of fun.
And you will go home knowing
and remembering,
that we ALL live under
the very same moon AND sun!

When you finally reach the dock.
Mom checks her watch for the time,
and NOT a clock.
Mom says, "We're early."
Dad says,
"It's better to be early than late!"
Then Mom looks up at him
and grumbles,
"Now for the train we'll HAVE to wait!"

As you leave the ferry
you see a bridge of blue,
that seems to talk and to beckon you.
And you remember,
that after all,
it's much better to build a bridge,
than to build a wall.

"We build too many walls and not enough bridges."

Isaac Newton

www.ingramcontent.com/pod-product-compliance
Ingram Content Group UK Ltd.
Pitfield, Milton Keynes, MK11 3LW, UK
UKHW060135240426
12048UKWH00002B/49